CURIOUS STORIES

OF FAMILIAR PLANTS FROM AROUND THE WORLD

By Kathy Keeler
A Wandering Botanist

AWanderingBotanist.com
Loveland, Colorado

Kathleen H. Keeler, A Wandering Botanist
2527 Indian Hills Drive
Loveland, Colorado 80538
www.AWanderingBotanist.com

Ordering Information:
Quantity Sales: Special discounts are available on quantity purchases by corporations, associations, and others. For details, contact the "Special Sales Department" at the address above or email Kathy@AWanderingBotanist.com

Photography: Kathleen H. Keeler

Curious Stories of Familiar Plants from Around the World
Kathy Keeler, A Wandering Botanist, 1st edition
ISBN 978-0-9861694-8-9

Conversions:
1 inch (1") is 2.54 centimeters.
1 foot (1') is approximately 0.3 meters.
1 mile is 1.6 kilometers.
1 pound is about 0.45 kilogram.
1 U.S. ton is 907 kilograms.
50 Fahrenheit is 10 Celsius; 80 Fahrenheit is 27 Celsius.

Table of Contents

Every day we are surrounded by plants gathered over thousands of years from all over the globe. They are familiar to us, so we hardly give them a thought. And yet, just as each of us can tell a story of how we came to be living where we are (the events that shaped our travels or our parents' or grandparents' travels), plants came here by strange paths, with interesting incidents along the way.

This book presents a few of the tales familiar plants could tell about where they came from, the folktales told about them, and the changes in their roles over time. I hope these articles will make you take a new look at familiar plants.

Wandering Watermelons

EVERYONE KNOWS WATERMELON, right? Big green fruit with red interior and black seeds. An essential part of American summer picnicking.

It came as a surprise to me that in China—not just in American Chinese restaurants—watermelon is the usual dessert. The meal ends when slices of watermelon are served.

It is a long way from Denver to Shanghai. Where is the watermelon from?

Wild watermelons (*Citrullus lanatus*, in the cucumber family, Cucurbitaceae) can readily be found in the deserts and semi-deserts of southern Africa. Consequently, Africa is believed to be where the plant first encountered people. Domestication of watermelons probably occurred in south or central Africa, but there is little record of it. What is known is that recognizable watermelons were portrayed in Egyptian paintings from as early as 3100-2180 BCE, and seeds were found in the tomb of King Tutankhamun (ca. 1330 BCE). Watermelons can be found in murals and mosaics at locations around the Mediterranean from the Roman era (510 BCE to about 410 CE) and in southern European medieval herbals 1200-1500 CE).

From Africa watermelons have been carried all over the world.

Not all of the watermelons of pre-modern Europe were our familiar sweet, red-fleshed watermelon. Although there are reportedly wild watermelons that are sweet, the majority of wild watermelons are quite bitter. These are often called citrons.

The name citron is shared between the bitter watermelon and a citrus fruit, the citron, *Citrus medica*, which can make it very hard to know which you are reading about. The citrus citron is a tree that produces a round fruit that looks a lot like a grapefruit (*Citrus x paradisi*). *Citrus medica* is a much older plant than the grapefruit. Citrons were domesticated prehistorically in Asia and reached Persia by 300 BCE. Grapefruits are derived from a mutant of the pomelo, *Citrus maxima*, that occurred about 1750 in Barbados. Citrus citrons are too bitter to eat fresh, so are mainly pickled. The other citron is a watermelon. One citron grows on a vine, the other on a tree; you wouldn't mix them up if the plant were present.

Both kinds of citron have been found in markets across Eurasia for centuries and were probably treated similarly by shoppers—taken home and pickled. Buying a citron by name at a market, especially in southern Italy or North Africa and possibly farther east, you could possibly get either a citrus fruit or a watermelon.

As late as the 1400s in Europe, many of the watermelons were citron melons, not sweet watermelons. In about half of the fourteenth- to sixteenth-century southern European manuscripts studied by H. S. Paris and collaborators, the watermelon shown is the citron melon.

Today citron melons are rarely cultivated or sold. They have, however, naturalized in the southern United States, where they can be found in waste places and as a crop weed.

Watermelons are first recorded as being in China in the tenth century. The Chinese name is *xīguā*, "western fruit," reflecting the idea that it is not native, but it has been there for 1,000 years now. As in the West, watermelons are very popular in China. Older reports describe diverse colors and sizes of watermelons in China, but today the familiar big red-fruited ones dominate. The Chinese love watermelon seeds as well as fresh watermelon. China produces the most watermelon in the world; watermelon production in 2010 was six times the production of the next four countries combined!

Watermelons were brought to the Americas soon after settlement. The earliest record is from Spanish Florida in 1576. By the 1600s watermelons can be documented all over North, Central, and South America, wherever the growing season is long enough.

Between citron melons and sweet watermelons, there were and are many interesting varieties of watermelon that are small to large, round to oval, with rinds from pale almost-yellow to deep green, with or without stripes, with flesh that is white, yellow, orange, or red and with seeds in colors from white to black. The taste, not the appearance, tells you that it is a watermelon and not some other kind of melon. See some of the variety at www. rareseeds.com.

The watermelons of my picnic and of the meal in Shanghai are both immigrants, originating long ago from the same source, and carried across the world by their fans.

Pomegranates in Story and History

A MYTH STARTED my research on pomegranates.

On a tour of Granada, Spain, the guides explained that Granada was named for pomegranates, *granada* in Spanish, and that the Moors had brought pomegranates to Spain.

I heard that as "the Moors brought pomegranates to Europe," and indeed it is stated that way in some history books. The Moors certainly introduced many Middle Eastern and Asian plants to Europe by planting them in Spain. But I knew that pomegranates played an important role in Greek mythology, so the Moors couldn't have brought pomegranates to Europe.

Pomegranates appear in mythology all over the Old World. Bright red flowers, delicious fruits full of seeds--everyone notices them.

Pomegranates are a backyard shrub if you live where there is virtually no frost, but they are an exotic fruit to people in climates with cold winters. The fruit ships well enough that northern grocery stores have had pomegranate fruits now and then as novelties for decades.

Pomegranates taste so good, they are responsible for winter.

Pomegranates have been cultivated since about 3,000 BCE. They apparently were domesticated from wild trees at the southern end of the Caucuses, and/or at the southern end of the Caspian Sea. There are still wild trees there. They appear to have been domesticated very long ago, at about the same time as dates, figs, grapes, and olives.

The Phoenicians may have taken the pomegranate to North Africa and the western Mediterranean. They can and do grow in Sicily, Mediterranean France, and southern Spain.

The scientific name is *Punica granatum*. Long separated into a family of their own (Punicaceae), pomegranates are now classified in the Lythraceae, the loosestrife family. The scientific name is based on the name used by the Roman writer Pliny. He called them *malus punica*, which is "Carthagean apple" or "apple from Carthage." Punic was the Latin adjective for the city of Carthage in north Africa and its surroundings, in what is today Tunisia. Rome imported pomegranates from Carthage, when they weren't at war. In the scientific name, *granatum* means "many-seeded," which pomegranates certainly are.

Our English common name, pomegranate, says the same thing. Pome is a Latin word for apple (or fruit), and there is *granate* again, "many-seeded."

Where do pomegranates appear in Old World mythology? Throughout the Middle East, but it is actually pretty frustrating to research, because mythology often produces just fragments of answers when you ask, "what are the oldest stories?" Zorastrian stories and ceremonies frequently include pomegranates. Founded by the prophet Zoraster of Persia (Iran) about 3,500 years ago, Zorastrianism is regarded as the first monotheistic religion and continues to be practiced in the Middle East and India. In the story of Zoraster's life, the Shah Gushtasp created his son Aspandiar an unbeatable warrior to fight for Zorastrianism by giving Aspandiar a pomegranate seed, which made his body "invulnerable as a stone."

Pomegranates were introduced to Egypt from Persia by at least the time of Thutmose III, 1,504-1,450 BCE. Egyptians embraced them, making them a symbol of prosperity and ambition. They were frequently painted on tomb walls and buried with the dead; clearly they were something you wanted in the afterlife.

The Hebrews knew pomegranates from Egypt. When Moses led them into the wilderness, they complained, "Why have you made us come up from Egypt, to bring us in to this wretched place? It is not a place of grain or figs or vines or pomegranates, nor is there water to drink." (Numbers 20:5) But Moses had sent scouts ahead who "came to the valley of Eshcol and from there cut down a branch with a single cluster of grapes; and they carried it on a pole between two men, with some of the pomegranates and the figs." (Numbers 13:23). Indeed, pomegranates grew in the Promised Land.

The Hebrews held pomegranates in high esteem. They were one of the Seven Species (with wheat, barley, grapes, figs, olives, and honey, staples of life). They were important offerings at the Feast of Tabernacles, in celebration of the harvest. Pomegranates alternated with golden bells on the robes of priests and were carved on the pillars at the doors to the temple in Jerusalem.

It was a story from ancient Greece that sent me on this chase, however. I knew that the Greeks knew about pomegranates, so the fruit must have been in Europe well before the Moors invaded Spain (8th century CE).

Not only do pomegranates appear in Greek mythology, but they are part of the explanation of why we have seasons.

Hades, god of the underworld, greatly desired and then kidnapped the goddess Persephone. Persephone was the daughter of Demeter, goddess of agriculture and the harvest. Devastated, Demeter put all her energy into finding her daughter. While she wandered distraught, crops failed.

The state of the world became desperate. Zeus, king of the gods, had to intervene. He told Hades to return Persephone.

However, in the underworld, Hades repeatedly tempted Persephone with delicious foods. Hades knew that if she ate something in the underworld, she had to stay. Persephone weakened, just once, and ate a pomegranate seed.

(I found versions of the myth that said one, four, six, or "some" seeds and could not find a version I thought most authentic. Note also a point that always bothered me: apparently, being a goddess, Persephone could survive for months without food. Or, she didn't need food in the underworld.)

But there was the rule: eating anything in the underworld committed one to staying there.

And yet the death of plants due to Demeter's distress was intolerable.

Seeking a solution, Zeus ruled that Persephone must spend part of each year with Hades. Thus, for part of the year Persphone is with her mother on earth, and for part of it she is with Hades in the underworld. While Persephone is with Hades every year, Demeter mourns and crops do not grow. The various versions of the story say there are four months of winter or six; the former is more appropriate for the climate of Greece. One month per seed seems harsh but fair to me, while several months or half the year seem an awfully stiff punishment for one pomegranate seed. On the other hand, she had eaten something and Zeus gave her an option that others wouldn't have gotten.

Whatever the details, eating a pomegranate seed, small but irresistibly delicious, explained winter in Greek cosmology.

In Roman mythology, Persephone is called Proserpina and Demeter is Ceres, but the story is essentially the same.

Granada, Spain, currently embraces the pomegranate, having it as the city's name and on its coat of arms. However, the city's early Moorish name was Karnattah (*Gharnāṭah*, thought to mean "hill of strangers"). That certainly sounds like, or could have morphed into, Granada, a familiar plant name. I think it's likely that the city of Granada adopted or was renamed for pomegranates, because it seems unlikely that Europeans forgot about pomegranates between the fall of Rome and the arrival of the Moors (maybe 400 years).

Across the world, pomegranates represent both fertility, from the number of seeds in the fruit, and the female body and/or birth, based on the red color. In modern Zorastrianism ceremonies, pomegranates represent the vegetable creation of god, as the egg represents the animal creation. Today pomegranates appear on Torah scrolls in remembrance of the temple and are commonly used when celebrating Rosh Hashanah because their many seeds are seen as corresponding to the Torah's 613 commandments. In Christianity, the red juice symbolizes the shed blood of Christ and the fruit is seen as the church holding within it all its people.

Pomegranates went east to China along the Silk Road in 135 CE. Zhang Qian, ambassador from the Han Chinese court to the Greco-Bactrian capital Kabul, carried a pomegranate tree to China when he returned home. He planted it in the Han capital Chang'an (now Xi'an). From there pomegranates were dispersed across Asia. The Chinese loved the red flowers and made them the subject of romantic poetry. The most inauspicious day of the Chinese year is the 5th day of the 5th month. Women traditionally wear pomegranate flowers on that day to ward off bad luck.

The shape of pomegranate fruits have had other curious influences —on crowns and bombs. The top of the fruit was reportedly the shape of the crown of Solomon, king of Israel (970-931 BCE). Subsequent crowns, including most of those in modern Europe, are frequently modeled after Solomon's crown. Pomegranates have also given their name to the grenade. The grenade, a small bomb that is thrown by hand, was developed for European warfare in the 15th and 16th centuries (although there were grenades before that in China and Byzantium). The French army called this weapon a pomegranate, *grenade* in French. The similarity is obvious: hand-sized and full of seeds, although the "seeds" in a hand grenade are deadly.

Pomegranates are novelty fruits in many places, but in the Middle East and India, they are important staples, used as spices or juices in cooking. Pomegranate concentrate is incorporated into Lebanese and Mediterranean sauces, soups, meat dishes, salads, and couscous. Dried seeds are a spice (*anardana*) for sweet-sour dishes in northwest India, especially Punjab and Gujarat. Grenadine is the syrup of pomegranates, used to add flavor or color to various alcoholic drinks. Pomegranate juice itself is a popular beverage from the eastern Mediterranean to India.

If you haven't eaten a pomegranate recently, take the next opportunity to do so!

Camellia and Tea

THERE HAVE BEEN TIMES when plant relationships surprised me. One of those cases is that tea is a camellia, or one kind of camellia gives us tea, whichever way you want to look at it.

When my father retired to Florida, he became a camellia grower, an officer in the local camellia society, and a judge at camellia flower shows. Consequently I learned a lot about camellias and certainly admired the flowers.

Camellia is a genus of shrubs, classified in the plant family Theaceae, native to east and southeast Asia, especially China and Japan. Camellias have attractive flowers and have been bred and hybridized to create great floral diversity. (To see some of the diversity, google the American Camellia Society webpage).

Camellias have been in cultivation in China and Japan for centuries. Most of the varieties cultivated for their flowers are *Camellia japonica*, although *Camellia reticulata* (from China) and *C. sassanqua* (from Japan) have contributed important varieties. The vast majority of the other species of camellia (104 to 248, depending on your botanical authority), are native to China, especially China south of the Yangtze River.

Camellias and tea are close relatives.

Camellias, at least the ones grown as ornamental shrubs for their flowers, require a moderate amount of moisture and do not tolerate heavy frost. Consequently, they are cultivated in the coastal United States and moist, mild parts of the rest of the world. All over the world you can see beautiful camellias grown for their flowers, from London to Melbourne, in Portland, Oregon and Atlanta, Georgia, and in Tokyo, Shanghai, and hundreds of places I've never been.

It came as a surprise to me, that teas (you know—Chinese tea, English breakfast tea, oolong, Earl Gray, and so on) are the leaves of a camellia, specifically *Camellia sinensis*.

The flowers of tea are considerably less attractive than those of the ornamental camellias and are generally ignored.

Tea is native to China. *Camellia sinensis* leaves are believed to have been brewed as tea (or chewed or pickled) for millennia in southern and western China and the adjacent countries of southeast Asia. The first written record of tea from China was about 2,737 BCE. Tea was clearly being cultivated all across China by 650 CE. Consequently it is difficult to know if wild *C. sinensis* still exists or if the apparently wild plants in China are descended from former plantings.

From China, tea drinking and cultivation spread around Asia. Early European navigators brought tea to Europe in the first years of the 17th century.

Like ornamental camellias, tea plants will grow into large shrubs or small trees. Cultivated tea plants are heavily pruned to keep them short.

Tea has been planted all over the world. Typical of camellias, it is intolerant of frost and so is confined to frost-free areas. However, tea grows best where temperatures do not exceed 85° F. Tea plants prefer at least 45 inches of rain a year and cannot survive if the monthly rainfall is less than about two inches for several months. That means that for all the tea that is grown in China, it only grows in southern China, generally in the mountains, and not, for example, near Beijing.

Tea is harvested by cutting the new leaves. This can be done as frequently as every two weeks if growing conditions are good. Processing depends on the type of tea being produced. Green teas are lightly steamed, dried, and rolled. For black teas, leaves are spread and withered to reduce the moisture in them, then rolled, crushed, and torn. These "disrupted" leaves are allowed to sit so the enzymes released by disruption ferment the leaf tissues, turning them brown. Finally, black tea is thoroughly dried. Oolong tea receives an intermediate treatment and is allowed to ferment only very slightly.

Most tea is drunk: after water it is probably the most widely consumed drink in the world. But in tea-growing regions, tea leaves are used in a variety of other ways. In 2007 in southern China, I was served tea leaves that had been flash-fried, I think, since they were crispy but not greasy. They were delicious.

It is hard to remember that tea is a camellia, because tea leaves and camellia flowers are used so differently.

Chocolate,
Food of the Gods

NO DOUBT YOU KNOW THE STORY OF CHOCOLATE.
My two favorite parts of the story are that it started out being drunk spiced with chilis, and that the name had to be changed.

Chocolate is made from the roasted seeds of a small tree, *Theobroma cacao*, in the plant family Sterculiaceae. It is native to the New World tropics, requiring warm temperatures (never below 60 F!) and plenty of rain. Big pods form on the branches of the tree. Unlike familiar temperate-zone fruit trees, the flowers and then the fruit (pods) of cacao come directly from the branches, not off little stems. That is probably important, considering that cacao pods are as big as grapefruits.

The original chocolate was a spicy, smelly drink that left your mouth bright red.

The plant is called cacao, not "chocolate tree." Cocoa, the last two letters reversed, refers to powdered chocolate. Other plants with similar names are coconuts and coca; neither is related to cacao. *Cocos nucifera* is the coconut palm, making coconuts. Cocaine, also called coca, comes from the plant *Erythroxylum coca* in the family Erythroxylaceae. It is not related to chocolate either.

Cacao has been cultivated for more than 2,000 years. It was important to the Maya and Aztecs, who used the beans as money and served the drink to their kings.

Cacao seeds are rich in fat (cocoa butter), which make ground seeds heavy, greasy, and insoluble in water. The ground seeds are bitter as well as rich. Changing both of these was needed to create the chocolate we recognize.

The Mayas and the Aztecs drank chocolate. With the natural cocoa-butter fats, it can be ground into a powder and suspended in liquid, but not formed into solid shapes. The traditional preparation required opening the pods and leaving the seeds to ferment in the air for several days. Then the beans were roasted and ground, and other ingredients were added. Cocoa powder was often served with local flowers, such as ear-flower (*Cymbopetalum penduliflorum*, custard-apple family, Annonaceae) and *mecaxochitl* (botanically *Piper sanctum*, a relative of black pepper). The drink could be dyed green or yellow, and spiced with additional leaves and seeds. Particularly popular, however, was to thicken it slightly with corn (maize) flour and flavor it with ground vanilla (*Vanilla planifolia*) and hot chili peppers (*Capsicum annuum*), then dye it red with achiote (*Bixa orellana*). The mixture was poured back and forth between containers to raise a thick foam, then it was drunk unheated. This was quite a different culinary experience from a milk chocolate candy bar.

The conquistadors who first encountered this drink found the foam rather repulsive, the taste bitter and the spices alien. And, the achiote stained the mouth and hands red. It did not take long for someone to add cane sugar and change the spices to cinnamon and anise seeds, providing a more familiar taste. The popularity of chocolate rose rapidly.

Initially supplies of cocoa reaching Europe were very limited. King Philip II of Spain (1527-1598), to whom the riches of the Americas flowed in great abundance in the 1500s, had to ration himself to a single cup of chocolate each night.

The Aztecs called the beverage they drank *cacahuatl*, meaning "cacao water" in their language, Nahuatl. When I first tried to use the term, it made me uncomfortable. In my childhood in New York City in the late 1940s, caca was a word for shit. For me the word still carries the discomfort that a young child feels about toilet training. The online English dictionaries today include caca, defined as excrement. And, in fact, caca is a word shared with the Romance languages. In Spanish, *caca* means shit. Sticking it on another word doesn't make it better. For example the modern Spanish dictionary has *caca-can*, pooper-scooper.

Imagine it is the year 1500 in Mexico. An acquaintance says, "Here, try this, it is called *cacahuatl*..."

And he offers you a bowl of peculiar-smelling thick brown liquid.

The origins of the word chocolate are obscure, likely from *cacao huatl*, same meaning but not using the usual Nahuatl word, but the importance of the change is really clear. Call it choco - not caca!!!

With an expanding market came greater production. Spain knew it had a good thing and tried to keep a monopoly on cacao, but by the middle of the 1600s the Dutch had plantations both in Curacao and in southeast Asia. Chocolate became available as a drink in most of Europe by the 1650s, moving from Spain, where it was popular in the court throughout the 16th century, to Italy, and from there to the rest of Europe.

For 200 years chocolate was a flavored, perfumed, fatty powder suspended in water. The changes that make the chocolate we recognize began in the early 1800s, when Dutch producers discovered how to remove much of the cocoa butter and added alkalai to neutralize the organic acids. The result was a milder, more soluble, less fatty drink. Twenty years later cocoa butter was successfully added back to the chocolate powder, allowing the production of chocolate candies. In the 1870s in Switzerland, Nestlé added condensed milk to make the first solid milk chocolate and Lindt discovered that stirring it continuously would create an extremely smooth, creamy texture. From those developments they could create all the forms of chocolate we eat today.

Native plants always have an array of enemies: insects, bacteria, viruses. Planting crops in regions where they are not native generally reduces the number of pests that attack the crop. That is why 70% of the world's chocolate is produced in the Ivory Coast, Ghana, and Indonesia. More than 4,000,000 tons of chocolate are produced annually, so a lot of chocolate produced in the Americas as well.

Now that it is such a popular food, we could probably call it cacahuatl and have no problem.

To taste something like the original cacahuatl of the Aztecs, try drinking mole sauce suspended in water. (see Notes)

In case you wondered, white chocolate is cocoa butter plus milk solids and sugar. And, "food of the gods" is the meaning of the scientific name *Theobroma*.

Writing is hungry work...where did I leave that chocolate bar?

Chrysanthemum, the Quintessential Plant of Fall

AS SUMMER FADES INTO FALL, a different set of plants dominate the landscape. In my garden, the chrysanthemums that were an unassuming cluster of leaves all summer are now covered in blossoms. My fruit trees are dropping peaches and apricots. Burning bush (*Euonymous*) and maples start to turn color. My garden is in Colorado, but those are Chinese plants or plants that are also found in China. In the late 1800s and early 1900s "plant hunters" searched East Asia for garden plants. Many familiar garden plants (lilacs, peonies, ever-blooming roses, nandina, butterfly bush) are native to China, introduced to the West by the plant hunters.

The Chinese believed that smelling chrysanthemums will extend your life.

Traditional Chinese culture noticed the progress of the seasons and cherished it. Plants were associated with seasons: plum blossoms for spring, orchids in summer, chrysanthemums with fall, bamboo in winter. These four were called The Four Gentlemen, also known as the Four Plants of Virtue. The Chinese believed that the right plant for the season was important and that having plants out of season brought bad luck.

Chrysanthemums (*jú* in Chinese) have been cultivated in China since 700 BCE. There, raising chrysanthemums has, for hundreds of years, been a respectable and desirable activity for retirees. Probably there is a double meaning here: flowers of autumn and the autumn of life.

Traditionally the Chinese used fragrant plants and flowers as indoor air fresheners. In fall they set out pots of chrysanthemums, indoors and in the courtyards of their homes, for just that purpose. Of course it brightened the spot, but in addition there was a long-held belief that the scent of chrysanthemums extended life. In that sense, chrysanthemum was the flower of immortality.

This level of interest in chrysanthemums produced thousands of shapes and colors; the shapes and colors of chrysanthemums in the West are only a small portion of those in China.

There are about 40 species in the genus *Chrysanthemum*, mainly in China. Despite their long history of cultivation there (chrysanthemum has been the national plant of Japan since 910 AD) chrysanthemums were first brought to Europe about 1680. These apparently died out. A reintroduction in the 1700s also died. About 1800 chrysanthemums became common European garden plants. The exact time of the introduction of "mums," to the United States is unclear, but it was probably about 1800.

The scientific name is confused because the first plant called *Chrysanthemum* was a small European flower. Later, Linnaeus added the plants from China and Japan to the genus *Chrysanthemum*. In 1961, a detailed analysis by the Russian botanist Tzvelev split the genus. The name *Chrysanthemum* went with that first flower and not with garden chrysanthemums (our mums). Eventually the International Association of Plant Taxonomists passed a rule giving the scientific name *Chrysanthemum* to the garden chrysanthemum. So chrysanthemums were *Dendranthema* species for about 30 years, but in 1995 they became

Chrysanthemum species again. A surprising number of the sites on the internet that talk about chrysanthemums still call them *Dendranthema*. As far as I can tell, all the *Dendranthema* species became *Chrysanthemum* species in 1995, so there no longer are any plants with the scientific name *Dendranthema*.

Chinese color symbolism is different from western color symbolism. First, white is strongly associated with death. Except at a funeral, do not give anyone white flowers in China. On the other hand, yellow, which has a lot of negative meanings in the West, was the Emperor's color and so had and has all kinds of strong, royal associations. Red for the

Chinese is the color of joy. Brides wear red to weddings. So for the Chinese, yellow and red chrysanthemums are for happy occasions.

In China as in eastern North America, fall brings colored leaves on the trees and in particular red maple leaves. The red maple leaf is another symbol of fall that we easily recognize.

What non-Chinese speakers don't see on an autumn-themed bowl or painting with a chrysanthemum and maple leaves is the pun. Chinese is rich in words with the same sound but different meanings. English has pair and pear, green plant and manufacturing plant, and my favorite: dye and die. ("My friend and I are dyeing today.")

Chrysanthemum, *jú* has nearly the same pronunciation as *jú*, which means entire or whole. Maple is *fēng*. *Fēng* also means lush, abundant. Consequently the phrase chrysanthemum maple, *jú fēng*, sounds like "abundant whole," that is, "live and work in peace and contentment."

Happy fall to you. Chrysanthemum and maple. *Jú fēng*.

Not Plain Vanilla

GOOD VANILLA IS ONE OF MY FAVORITE FLAVORS, and the idea of "plain vanilla," or vanilla as a no-flavor flavor, has always annoyed me, because vanilla really is a flavor.

Vanilla is native to the Americas and did not reach Europe until after 1492. At that time it was a rare and highly desirable flavor.

Vanilla comes from long, thin bean-like pods, but vanilla is not at all a bean (beans are usually legumes, plant family Fabaceae), but is an orchid (plant family Orchidaceae). In fact, it is the only orchid used as a food or commercially sold in any way other than as an ornamental (flower), even though there are more species of orchids than species in any other plant family, even legumes or grasses.

Vanilla is the only orchid eaten as food.

Vanilla is a climbing vine with fleshy leaves longer than my hand, and two to three fingers wide. We grew a vanilla orchid in the greenhouse at the University of Nebraska; it climbed up to the ceiling. Then the stem planted in the pot broke, so the plant was hanging from the wall and ceiling without being rooted in soil at all. It lived like that for years. The flowers of the vanilla orchid are cream-colored, recognizable as orchid flowers. The fruit develops as long dark pods. As is typical with orchids, the seeds inside the pods are tiny, but the pod around the seeds grows to be several inches long. This is what forms the spice vanilla. The fruit takes about nine months to mature. The pod with mature seeds smells and tastes nothing like vanilla until it has fermented. In vanilla production, pods are dried in the sun for up to four hours, then wrapped in airtight boxes to sweat. This may be repeated daily for up to a month. Then they are dried indoors for a month and conditioned for another three months. I presume that the people who discovered vanilla picked up fermenting pods on the forest floor.

Current taxonomy recognizes 103 species of vanilla, genus *Vanilla*. The major species in cultivation is *Vanilla planifera*, which is native to Mexico.

Vanilla was an important ingredient in the chocolate eaten by the Aztecs. Cortez and his men or, alternately, settlers in Cuba sent vanilla beans (as well as cacao, chili peppers and cochineal dye) home to Spain, probably by 1510. The very first vanilla to arrive was described as a perfume, but it was soon used as a flavoring. The *Codex Barberini*, called the *Badianus Manuscript*, an Aztec herbal from 1552 written by Martius de la Cruz in Latin, clearly describes it. Franciscan

Friar Bernardino de Sahaguin, who went to Mexico in 1529, popularized the use of vanilla in his *Florentine Codex: General history of the things of New Spain*, published in Spain in 1560.

The Aztecs called it *tlilxochitl*. Our name for vanilla is from *vainilla*, "little pod," based on the Spanish word *vaina*, "pod." By the second half of the 16th century, the Spanish had the Indians in Mexico harvesting, fermenting, and drying vanilla for export to Europe to be used with chocolate. The Spanish name was disseminated to Europe along with the product. It was a rare and extremely expensive spice.

The earliest use of vanilla alone is credited to Hugh Morgan, an English pharmacist at the court of Elizabeth I. In 1602 Morgan reportedly tried vanilla alone in candies. The Queen liked it and thereafter consumed a lot of vanilla. For the English generally, vanilla became popular later in the 17th century, presumably as supplies increased.

Vanilla was recognized as a desirable crop early in the 1500s and plants were successfully transplanted to tropical countries all over the world. However, no vanilla was produced. In its native forests, vanilla is pollinated by very specific insects. As late as 1971 the pollinators of orchids had not been identified. We now know they are stingless *Melipona* bees (I've worked a little with *Melipona* in Costa Rica; they're cute). Without these bees carrying pollen between flowers, vanilla will not produce seeds or pods. Not only that, a particular species of bee is required for a particular species of vanilla orchid. At the time that vanilla was transplanted around the world, science did not understand plant reproduction and could not explain why vanilla production failed. It was not until the 1760s that botanists began to figure out how insect pollination of flowers worked. Hand pollination of vanilla in Madagascar successfully produced pods there. Even today, hand pollination is used to ensure adequate pollination of vanilla flowers. Hand pollination is slow work, which is part of the reason for the continued high price of natural vanilla. Natural vanilla, made from fermented pods, includes tiny black vanilla seeds and can be easily distinguished from products made with vanilla extract or artificial vanilla.

Vanilla availability gradually improved as vanilla plantations around the world, especially in Madagascar and Oceania, produced vanilla. Extracting the flavor into alcohol in vanilla extract (1847), allowed even easier use of vanilla flavor in cooking. In 1874 German chemists synthesized vanillin, the most important compound in vanilla. Vanillin can be made from a variety of natural materials, including wood pulp. This dramatically reduced the cost of vanilla flavor and created "plain vanilla," which denoted the bland "default" flavor.

It isn't necessary to settle for plain vanilla, however. Natural vanilla is still available, still expensive, and a much more complex and interesting flavor than synthetic vanilla.

Holly, Celebrating the Solstice and Christmas for Millennia

WE SING "DECK THE HALLS WITH BOUGHS OF HOLLY" at Christmastime, often without thinking about what we are saying.

I live in an area where the traditional holly cannot grow, and yet everyone knows what holly looks like.

Why?

Holly is the common name of most of the plants in the genus *Ilex* in the holly family, Aquifoliaceae. It is an interesting family because, while there are 450 species in the Aquifoliaceae, each and every one is an *Ilex*. All the plants are in one genus, yet in a distinct family, indicating that the hollies are all quite similar to each other, and yet a distinctive and recognizable group that is not very like any other living plant. The similarities mean that although hollies can be trees, shrubs, and occasionally vines, and some hollies have orange or black fruits as well as red fruits, if you encounter a new holly, you are apt to be struck by the similarity and think "that reminds me of holly."

In addition, *Ilex* species are scattered all over the world, on every continent except Antarctica (which really means all continents, since there are no higher plants in Antarctica). Hollies are apparently an old group that spread all over the world more than 90 million years ago. Their near relatives have died out.

The holly that everybody knows is *Ilex aquifolium*, European holly. It is native to southeastern Europe, but spread to the British Isles and across northern Europe prehistorically. Probably humans carried some of the fruits, but undoubtedly birds did too. The red drupes (properly, holly berries are called drupes; see Notes) are slightly toxic to humans but they are very edible to birds. Holly was then carried all over the world and you can find it in suitable climates from Australia to the United States, both planted and escaped (it is a serious weed in California).

In addition to having clusters of bright red drupes, each almost as large as a blueberry, European holly is broad-leafed evergreen. Evergreen means the plant's leaves stay green throughout the winter (or where there is no winter, in the dry season). The largest group of evergreens in the Northern Hemisphere are coniferous trees. Their needle-like leaves endure frost particularly well and remain on the tree all year, while the leaves of oaks and maples turn colors and then fall.

Because European holly is evergreen, it stands out and demands attention in winter. When other broad-leaved trees are leafless, holly is leaf-covered and green. Not just green, shiny green. And don't forget red fruit. Holly has shiny green leaves and big red drupes to brighten your winter.

Of course people love it in winter—a splash of green and red on a brown or white landscape. We know the Romans gathered boughs of holly for their winter solstice celebration, Saturnalia. It seems likely that earlier and less well-documented cultures celebrated midwinter with holly as well.

Northern European pagans loved holly. Druids made wreaths for their heads. They grew the trees near their homes because they believed that faeries lived in, or were kept safe in, holly trees.

Folk beliefs that are probably from pagan times were carried forward. For example, holly wood was supposed to protect children and animals by keeping unfriendly spirits away. A holly, not planted but having arrived on its own, growing close to the house, guarded the inhabitants from witches. It also kept the inhabitants safe from fire, lightning, and nightmares.

European Christians saw the same virtues in the holly—green and red in a bleak winter landscape—and incorporated it into Christmas festivities. After centuries of celebrating Christmas with holly, since there are few places in Europe where it doesn't grow, there is a rich tradition of holly folklore. In fact, in parts of England the common name for holly is simply Christmas.

Christian holly folklore states that holly springs up in Jesus' footprints. (This is symbolic; I cannot find that it grows in the Holy Land). The rest of the Christian symbolism is clear; its spiny green leaves represent the crown of thorns, the red fruit recall blood and passion, the white flowers Christ's purity, and the very bitter bark suffering.

Holly folklore made it very bad luck to cut the tree except right at Christmas or to have it indoors except at Christmas, and in some places, not even then. While breaking off branches was limitedly acceptable, cutting them would bring bad luck and people who cut down healthy holly trees were reported to have died within the year, even though they had been perfectly healthy.

In contrast, in Scotland, if a young woman silently gathered a sprig of holly leaves on Christmas Eve, tied it in a three-cornered handkerchief, and slept with it under her pillow that night, she would see her future husband in her dreams.

In the 20th century, Harry Potter's personal magic wand was made of holly wood.

Handle your holly with care and enjoy its holiday folklore and symbolism.

Curiously, although European holly is widely recognized by its spiny leaves and red drupes, not all the leaves on European holly are spiny and not all the plants have fruit.

First, the number of spiny leaves on holly trees vary. You can see it in the photos; some leaves are smooth and others have spines on the edge.

All sorts of people have measured the variation in the spines. Young plants tend to have mostly spiny leaves. On a big tree, the lower branches have more spiny leaves than higher branches. The explanation appears to be that the spines deter browsing by big animals—deer for example. If protected from browsing, for example inside a fence, the plants will have mostly spineless leaves. But the regrowth after a deer or cow has eaten a number of leaves will have mainly spiny leaves. The little plant in the photo is not knee-high, so it is quite vulnerable to animals and its leaves are almost entirely very spiny.

Folklore acknowledged the variation in spines, and it was important to bring in both smooth and prickly leaves for Christmas decoration. If prickly came in first, the husband would rule the house for the year; if smooth, then the wife would rule.

Despite the variation, the leaves with their points are very distinctive and are an important part of the way people around the world recognize holly. Indeed, many other plants are described as having holly-like leaves: holly-leafed cherry *Prunus ilicifolia* (*ilic-* from *Ilex* holly, *-folia* meaning leaf), holly-leafed banksia (*Banksia ilicifolia*), and holly-leafed mangrove (*Acanthus ilicifolium*) are examples of this. However, the holly oak (*Quercus ilex*) of the eastern Mediterranean is not named after holly, but vice-versa; the *Ilex* of the oak was taken by Linnaeus to be the genus name of holly.

The holly tree is known as Christmas in parts of England.

The second easily recognizable characteristic of hollies—the red fruit—also varies among plants. European holly is dioecious, so only half the trees produce fruit. That is, there are female fruit-bearing plants and male plants that produce pollen but not fruit. (It's not rigorously correct to write male and female for plants, but it gets the idea across quickly). The very big holly at the Chelsea Physic Garden in London, shown below, is male and produces no fruit.

One consequence of dioecy is that if you want holly for the bright red fruit, you have to plant at least two, because without a male to contribute pollen, the female tree won't be fertilized and so will not develop any fruit. And because there is no way to know from a seed whether it is male or female, planting more than two will increase the odds of having both sexes.

The white flowers are pretty and attract bees. Of course, a neighbor's hollies can pollinate yours or vice versa.

Many species of holly such as those native to cooler parts of North America (possum haw *Ilex decidua* and winterberry *Ilex verticillata*), are deciduous, not evergreen, and lose their leaves in winter. They are still easy to love for the red drupes and the birds they attract, but it is a different look.

Holly, Postscript

In researching European holly *Ilex aquifolium* I generated questions; here are the answers to two that puzzled me:

1) Is the word holly derived from holy?

and

2) Is Hollywood, California, named for a grove of European holly trees?

1) Is the word holly derived from holy?

Although it seems logical that the word holly is a version of holy, and although holly has for hundreds of years been a part of midwinter religious celebrations by both Christians and pagans, there is no relation between the two words, which have different origins. Holly is from Old English *holen, holegn*, from *hollin*, which means the holly plant, as far back as it can be traced. Holy, on the other hand, is from Old English *hálig*, which means inviolate, inviolable.

2) Is Hollywood, California, named for a grove of European holly trees?

When googling the word holly, the city Hollywood often came up. However, European holly would have had to be imported and planted in southern California by the 1870s for the town to have been built in or near a holly wood. That seemed unlikely and sent me in pursuit of the relationship of holly to Hollywood.

There are several theories of how Hollywood, California, was named, and three different people have been given credit. What I was trying to work out is not WHO named it Hollywood, but WHY it was named Hollywood. Were there hollies there?

Some websites suggest that Hollywood, California, was named for either Hollywood, Illinois (now Brookfield, Illinois) or Hollywood, Florida. That doesn't work: Hollywood, California is older than the other two; Hollywood, California was incorporated in 1887, Hollywood Illinois, in 1893, and Hollywood Florida, in the 1920s.

Hollywood is named after a California native plant.

H.H.Wilcox registered the name in California in 1887. He reported that his wife suggested the name. The story is that, crossing the country, Daeida Wilcox met a woman on the train who had a summer home in Hollywood, Illinois. Liking the name, when she returned to California she named her property Hollywood. However, as far I can tell there was no Hollywood, Illinois, in the 1880s (see above). That doesn't preclude someone there area naming their home Hollywood. But why would they have done that? The only holly that can grow in Hollywood, Illinois is American holly, *Ilex opaca*, which might have occurred in bottomlands around Chicago. But Chicago is at the northern tip of American holly's range and was prairie before settlement, with very few trees. Currently it is hard to grow any kind of holly in Chicago. However, none of that prevents Mrs. Wilcox from being inspired by something in the conversation and applying the name Hollywood to her land in California. But why did she choose holly?

The Father of Hollywood website argued that H. J. Whitley, southern California developer, named Hollywood while on his honeymoon in 1886. The website said:

> "[When] HJ Whitley came to California in the late 1800s he stood on a hillside overlooking a fertile valley of orchards and farms and dreamed of what he could develop here.

> "It was at that moment that a Chinese immigrant approached driving a wagon pell mell towards the Whitleys. Whitley asked, "What are you doing here?" The Chinese man answered in broken English, "Work hard, hauley wood." There he sat in a wagon full of wood being hauled to town. And that is how the "Entertainment Capital of the World" got its name!" (Jan 22, 2011 entry)

That is very cute, but I found Whitley's wife's actual diary online and in it Gigi Whitley told the story a little differently, and spelled it "holly." So I'll offer an alternative, that the Chinese immigrant, John, said that his wagon was loaded with holly wood.

The name Hollywood is also attributed to Ivar Weid, a Dane who settled in the area in the 1860s. In the piece of Mrs.

Whitley's diary online, her husband proposed to go to Weid and develop the area with him, which suggests they agreed on the name.

Likely, as Water and Power Associates' history the name idea was Whitley's, Weid liked it, Mrs. Wilcox learned of it from Weid, and her husband registered it, in 1887.

But again, why holly?

In the 1880s, the area that became Hollywood, California was close to Holly Canyon. Older than Hollywood, Holly Canyon no longer exists; it was flooded to form Lake Hollywood in the 1920s.

Why was the canyon called Holly Canyon?

English holly (*Ilex aquifolium*) has been introduced to California, but without irrigation, the area around Hollywood is too dry for it. None of the native American hollies, genus *Ilex*, are native in California.

The answer is a similar-looking species, native to California.

Almost certainly Holly Canyon was named for the quite spectacular California holly, also called Christmas berry, and today known as toyons, *Heteromeles arbutifolia*. Despite the small red fruits and evergreen leaves, toyons are not related to European holly but rather to roses.

Toyons are native only to California. They can grow to be 20' trees, though that is uncommon. They make spectacular displays of evergreen leaves and red berries (pomes, like tiny apples, actually) that would have very much impressed settlers in California. (Google toyons to see wonderful photos.) They were common in the California hills and probably grew abundantly in and on Holly Canyon.

All the namers of Hollywood would have seen the hollies (toyons) of Holly Canyon and would have found the name both appropriate and appealing. I find it very satisfying that the holly that Hollywood is named for is a native California plant.

The Coconuts of Medieval Iceland

A COCONUT IN ICELAND? In the Middle Ages?

I'm sure I could find one in the market in Reykjavik today. Coconuts are tropical, but lots of tropical things are traded all over the world. For example, Icelandic chocolate is a favorite across all Scandinavia, even though chocolate is produced from plants that do not grow in Iceland. Coconuts are native far, far from Iceland.

Coconuts are the seeds of the coconut palm, *Cocos nucifera* (palm family, Arecaceae). Palms, like bananas and bamboo, are not strictly trees, because they do not form wood. The tough and flexible coconut palm trunk is made of the very tightly overlapping bases of the large leaves. Coconut palms can grow as tall as 80 feet.

The word coconut is used for the plant, the fruit, and the seed. I'll try to be clear.

Coconut fruits have a thick green covering surrounding a single, hard, nut-like seed. Inside the coconut seed is the embryo and coconut water (liquid endosperm) to feed the developing seedling. Over time, the endosperm solidifies into an oil-rich layer inside the seed coat, the "coconut" that we eat in chunks or grate in cooking. When the fruit is ripe, the outer green covering turns yellow, orange, red, or brown.

A mature coconut fruit is 8 to12 inches long. A full-sized coconut fruit can weigh 4.4 pounds.

As noted above, coconut palms are tropical, growing in the oceanic coasts of the tropics. They are believed to be native to the Indo-Pacific; that is, in the area of Malaysia and Indonesia. From there they dispersed east into the South Pacific and west toward Africa. Coconuts float well and can drift across large areas of open ocean to germinate on new shores, but long ago, humans found coconuts extremely useful and helped coconuts reach new lands. Before

Columbus, they grew pretty much all around the Indian and Pacific Oceans, but were not found in the Atlantic.

European culture, developing on the Atlantic Ocean and the Mediterranean Sea, knew nothing of coconuts for hundreds of years. Before Portuguese explorers crossed the equator off Africa in the 1480s, only a handful of Europeans had traveled to Asia, seen the Indian Ocean, or visited tropical east Africa, and even fewer had returned. Marco Polo wrote about a coconut he saw in 1280 in Sumatra. Coconuts, the de-husked shell of the seed, were probably occasionally brought by traders into the southern Mediterranean, but after 1300, tensions between Christians and Moslems impeded overland trade with the East.

Consequently, the coconut was one of the strange fruits discovered by Portuguese explorers when they sailed south around Africa. By 1550, European sailors had carried coconuts to Brazil and the Caribbean. They also took them home to Europe. As early as 1498, Vasco da Gama brought coconuts from India to Europe, where they were a sensation!

Some of the coconuts that sailed around Africa in European ships probably were in good condition upon arrival in Portugal. But after the milk was drunk and the meat eaten, the shell still had value. Coconut-shell cups became the rage among the wealthy in Europe in the 1500s. They set the homely brown shells in fine silver and used them as drinking goblets.

That is why there is a 500-year-old coconut in the National Museum of Iceland. The St. Nicholas Chalice is dated at about 1500 CE. It was a possession of the Church of St. Nicholas at Oddi, Iceland, a famous center of learning in

Iceland from the 11th century. Bound in silver, embellished with gilt filigree, and set with colored stones or equally valuable glass, the coconut in the St. Nicholas Chalice was used to commemorate the saints on holy days.

There was indeed at least one coconut in medieval Iceland.

The Exquisite Lotus

"AS A LOTUS FLOWER IS BORN IN WATER, grows in water and rises out of water to stand above it unsoiled, so I, born in the world, raised in the world having overcome the world, live unsoiled by the world," wrote Siddhartha

Gautama Buddha. Thus, the lotus is an important symbol in Buddhism.

Buddha's imagery is an accurate description of the life of the lotus plant.

Lotus, also called the sacred lotus, *Nelumbo nucifera* (lotus family, Nelumbonaceae) has been grown across Asia since prehistoric times. Not only a beautiful flower, it is also an important food plant; the leaves, rhizomes (roots), and seeds are edible.

Lotuses grow happily in deep mud. The lotus pond is likely to be a stinky spot that will cover you in thick, reeking mud if you venture there. And yet, out of that rises the lotus, with a perfectly gorgeous flower.

Lotus is an ancient plant. Recognizable fossils date back to the age of dinosaurs (Upper Cretaceous), but it went extinct in large parts of the world and its current distribution undoubtedly reflects its importance to humans.

The lotus is unique. Only two living species are recognized and are the sole members of the plant family Nelumbonaceae, the lotus family. One species of lotus, *Nelumbo lutea*, is native to North America, although it is not well-known to North Americans. In Asia, everyone knows the other species of lotus, the sacred lotus, *Nelumbo nucifera*.

Under growing conditions it likes, the sacred lotus can spread rapidly. In India, for example, when the rains fill dry low spots, the return of the lotus from mud-buried rhizomes can be so fast as to seem miraculous.

The leaves can grow to be three feet across.

The flowers are insect-pollinated and have an attractive scent. The flowers of the sacred lotus range from white to pink to red to pale yellow. *Nelumbo lutea*, the American or yellow lotus, has yellow flowers.

The sacred lotus is tropical, tolerating frost only if it is growing in deep enough water so that it doesn't freeze. As a rooted aquatic, the lotus needs to grow from the mud on the bottom to the surface, so really deep ponds are too deep for it to reach the surface. The result is that you don't generally find sacred lotuses in a cold climate. Bringing the plants indoors in winter or replanting in the spring allows them to be grown in most places.

The sacred lotus is so dramatic and beautiful that it is an important religious symbol to Buddhists, Hindus, Jains, Taoists, and Shintos and probably others. Scholars suspect that the lotus was the symbol of the mother goddess of the people who lived in India before the Aryans arrived. Native Americans found mystic powers in the equally glorious American lotus.

The image of the lotus rising out of the muck, spectacularly beautiful and wonderfully fragrant, is easy to cherish. The lotus repeats it in pond after pond, year after year.

Common Houseleek and Its Folklore

ONE WIDELY PLANTED SUCCULENT is the plant I grew up calling hens-and-chickens, *Sempervivum tectorum* (Crassulaceae, stonecrop family). These days the preferred common name is houseleek. There are 34 genera and 1,400 species in the Crassulaceae, with 30 species of

Sempervivum and hundreds of *Sempervivum* hybrids and cultivated varieties. *Sempervivum tectorum* thus gets called the common houseleek, since you might want to call all the other sempervivums houseleeks too.

Native to Europe, the common houseleek has grown in and around human settlements for a very long time. Like many plants that are familiar to a lot of people, it has many common names. Frequently used in the United States are hens-and-chickens and common houseleek. More obscure common names are Aaron's rod, bullock's eye, Jupiter's beard, Thor's beard, syngreen, and a half-dozen more (for more examples, see Wikipedia).

The scientific name, *Sempervivum* means "live forever" (*semper* = always, *vivum* = living), as does the common name syngreen and its variants. This doubtless refers to the fact that uprooted plants can survive for weeks, living on their stored water. Pluck a pansy (*Viola tricolor*) or a dandelion (*Taraxacum officinale*), with or without roots, and in hours they are wilted and in a day or two, dead. Do the same thing to a rosette of hens-and-chickens, and more than a week later you can stick it back in moist soil and it will recover. Try it!

This is the benefit of storing water the way a succulent does.

The hens-and-chickens common name follows from the growth form, where little clones grow around the initial plant. (See picture above.)

The *tectorum* in *Sempervivum tectorum* and the English names Jupiter's beard, Thor's beard and houseleek all refer to the plant's long association with lightning.

This is a story that seems very odd to us in the modern world. First, the plant was called Jupiter's beard (*Iovis barbam*) in ancient Rome. As I understand it, most Roman men were clean-shaven. Jupiter, king of the gods and king of the sky, was routinely pictured with a beard. The round shape of *Sempervivum tectorum*, native to the Alps and the Pyrenees, reminded Romans of the face of Jupiter. From that, somehow, came the belief that the plant, Jupiter's beard, would protect them from the lightning they believed was cast by Jupiter—perhaps simply because the plant was associated with Jupiter, or perhaps because the plant was moist and succulent.

Lightning strikes were as frightening to Romans as they are today. In fact, they were perhaps more frightening because to them, lightning was a completely mysterious force. There was no explanation linking lightning to anything familiar to Romans. Consider that electricity was unknown to science until the 1700s, and was an obscure scientific curiosity until after Edison made electric lights practical (1880s). In classical Rome, an inexplicable force from the sky struck a house and the house burned to the ground before neighbors could organize a bucket brigade from the creek.

This probably led to a variety of superstitious practices now lost to history. Planting *Sempervivum tectorum* on the roof to ward off lightning, however, was definitely a Roman response to the threat of lightning. That is easier to comprehend if you imagine sod or thatched roofs in Europe, rather than modern shingled roofs. Planting on roofs is the origin of *tectorum*, which translates to "of roofs." It is believed to also be the origin of the name houseleek. Houseleek means "house plant." Leek, and spelling variants such as leac, is an old Anglo-Saxon word for plant, most often seen in garlic (garlaec). Thus, houseleek is the plant on the house. (Before the development of clear glass windows, in the seventeenth century, plants could not grow indoors, so our current use of the term houseplant, a plant grown inside the house, is from after the advent of glass windows.) People believed houseleeks on the roof would protect them from lightning. Likewise they believed houseleeks would protect the house from fire. It does seem reasonable that the succulent leaves might not catch fire as easily as, say, grass on the roof.

This practice was preserved for historians when Charlemagne (720-814), first Holy Roman Emperor and unifier of a large part of northern Europe, ordered that all villagers within his crown lands plant houseleeks on their roofs, presumably as a safety measure. He decreed: *Et ille hortulanus habeat super domum suam Iovis barbam.* ("And the gardener shall have house-leeks growing on his house." *Capitulare de villis*, about 795, LXX.) Note that Charlemagne used the name Jove's—Jupiter's—beard.

Europeans grew houseleeks to protect their homes from lightning.

Thor's beard is also an English common name for the plant. That would be a reasonable name to have been used by the pagan Germanic tribes with whom Charlemagne interacted, although I don't actually find it in late medieval English herbals (Culpeper, Gerard, Hill, see Sources). Our English days of the week, for example, Thursday, Thor's day, come from the names of the gods of the Germanic Anglo-Saxon tribes who settled in England beginning in the fifth century. Charlemagne fought Germanic pagans and is famous for forcibly converting them to Christianity. Charlemagne lived before the time of Viking raids. Those began in his grandson's time. The name Jupiter's beard is therefore older than the Viking era, though it may have been in use by German pagans.

Lightning and fires are still threats. Wild fires sweep through the western United States most summers. People living in those areas are advised by their fire departments to landscape to reduce the risk of fire damage. For example, Susan Clotfelter in the *Denver Post* suggested planting fire-wise plants such as sedums, echinacea, and flax. I would add common houseleeks to a fire-resistant garden, if only for historical interest.

A World of Bananas

BANANAS DOMINATE THE WORLD'S FRESH-FRUIT TRADE.

Mostly, Banana plants cannot survive a touch of frost, and yet banana fruits are found in markets all over the world, in the depths of winter. More bananas are traded internationally than any other fruit, selling 30% more tons than apples, the next-most-traded fruit.

Bananas have been grown by people for thousands of years, likely almost 7,000 years. They are native to southeast Asia, but were so long ago domesticated, hybridized, and traded that even the experts say that "No good dates can be assigned to the early evolution and migrations of bananas." (Simmonds, p. 372). They were spread across Asia and the Pacific islands long ago and reached Africa maybe 2,000 years ago. Bananas grown in northern Africa were eaten in ancient Rome.

Early in the 16th century, bananas were first planted in tropical America. There they had no natural enemies and grew very well indeed. Today, South and Central America dominate world banana exports.

Banana plants are called trees, but they are really just very big herbs. The botanical distinction is that trees have wood, a complex and particular structure. Bananas do not. Banana plants can grow very tall (27 feet), but the trunk that supports them is a pseudostem (technical term) formed of the rolled bases of all the leaves.

Banana leaves can be impressively large, to nine feet long and two feet wide.

Centuries ago, growers developed plants with the seeds so reduced that they are just dark dots in the white fruit. Lacking seeds, cultivated bananas have to be propagated from suckers or cuttings. This has the benefit of creating uniform fruit quality and the disadvantage of making all the plants susceptible to the same diseases because they are genetically identical (clones).

Defining the species of a long-domesticated plant grown from clones is difficult. Certainly, they are in the genus *Musa*, a genus of about 40 species in the banana family,

Musaceae. Most commonly cultivated bananas are called *Musa acuminata* and *M. balbisiana* or their hybrid, *Musa paradisiaca*. Additional species are cultivated in Asia.

Bananas are monocotyledons, in the same major plant group as grasses. Visualizing them as huge tropical grasses is, while probably horrifying to a botanical purist, a whole lot closer to the situation than thinking of them as trees such as apple, oak, or banyan (fig).

The flowering stalk first develops a set of male flowers, which in the wild held pollen. In cultivated plants, those flowers are sterile and the pollen, if any, never matures. After the male flowers come female flowers with ovaries for making fruit. These are closer to the ground than the male flowers initially, but the big flower stalk almost always bends over, putting the female flowers higher in the air, above the male flowers. The female flowers develop into fruit parthenogenetically, meaning without being fertilized.

Banana terminology is fun. The big bunch of fruit is called a "stem." Within the stem (bunch) a cluster of fruits is a "hand." Within the hand, individual fruits are called "fingers." A bunch can contain several hands and each hand can have more than a dozen fingers. Don't miss telling someone you are eating a finger next time you bite into a banana.

The importance of bananas is hard to overstate. They are the number-one fruit traded in the world. They are essential to the economies of the countries that are major world banana exporters; for example, Ecuador, the Philippines, Costa Rica, Colombia, and Guatemala. (The data I have is from 2013 and the market shares are changeable). Bananas are one of the most profitable items in grocery stores in the United States and Europe, and therefore make a substantial contribution to store income.

Banana plants grow 20' tall but are not trees.

Bananas are critically important across Africa, although Africa doesn't export many bananas. Africans eat more bananas per capita than anyone else in the world. They grow multiple varieties and use them raw, cooked, and fermented as beer.

Bananas are nutritious. They contain a good combination of sugars and starches, as well as being a reliable source of potassium and vitamin C. Another virtue of banana plants is that they produce fruit all year long. Not only that, banana plants produce more fruit per plant than just about any other plant.

There are hundreds of varieties of banana, differing in firmness, starchiness, sweetness, etc. Consequently bananas are eaten fresh (as a fruit, in salads, in desserts), fried, baked, roasted, cooked into desserts, and more. Simply mashed, they make excellent baby food.

We get very few banana varieties in the northern United States. We call bananas that will be eaten fresh "bananas," and call the starchy ones to be cooked "plantains." However, the distinction works only when you have just a couple of banana varieties. Many banana varieties can be eaten and enjoyed either fresh or cooked.

The Oxford English Dictionary reports the word banana as coming into English from Portuguese or Spanish, both of which say banana, and, according to the OED, it came from the name used in Guinea (Congo) in Africa. Most European languages say some form of the word banana. And yet, it is *ndizi* in Swahili, *dikó:ndi* in the Munukutuba language of the Congo-Brazzaville, *banana* in Wolof of Senegal, *pisang* in Malay, *kluai* in Thai, *banana* in Javanese, *kelaa* in Hindi, *mai'a* in Hawaiian, *jiao* in Chinese and *banana* in Japanese. The trail of the name around the world may be as interesting as the path of the plants.

Whatever you call them, bananas are a popular, versatile fruit worldwide.

But that's not all:

What plant should no garden be without?

A banana plant. For a traditional Chinese garden, it's a must.

As far north as they will survive in China, every garden has one.

But not for the fruit.

The traditional Chinese garden grows bananas for the leaves.

71

For the shape of the leaves, but even more for the whisper of wind in the leaves and the tapping of raindrops on the leaves.

In September of 2010 my husband and I took a day trip from Shanghai to Suzhou, to see the famous classical gardens there. The Garden of the Master of Nets is famed for creating beauty and diversity within a small space. Many Chinese gardens in Europe and the United States are based upon it. In the Garden of the Master of Nets, the paths turned frequently to provide continuously changing views of the garden. It was exquisite.

Our visit to the garden was very wet. It rained or drizzled the whole day, which means I got to experience "wet poetry," or a garden in the rain. And to hear the patter of raindrops on banana leaves.

Of course rain is frequent in the productive regions of China, so they built gardens with shelters in them, to read or write comfortably on a rainy day. A traditional Chinese garden is more than a collection of plants. It includes halls, some wide open, some mostly enclosed, for entertaining or contemplation, the rooms an integral part of the garden. The sound of the rain is part of the experience. Raindrops on banana leaves make a distinctive sound, reverberating on the big leaves, so banana plants are essential.

Chinese gardens grow bananas for the sound of them.

Chinese and Japanese gardeners like the flowers, don't say much about the fruit, but have extolled the leaves in poetry and prose since at least the Tang Dynasty (6th century CE).

Li Ching Chao (1084-1150 CE) wrote:

> *I planted a banana tree outside the window, and already*
> *its shade fills the courtyard,*
> *its shade fills the courtyard.*
> *Leaf after leaf, heart after heart*

so full of feeling, some furled and some open
in third-watch rain, it is wounding a heart among pillows
drop by drop of icy clarity,
drop by drop of icy clarity,
with grief, and ruin, a far-off stranger
who can't get used to the sound.

In Japan, Basho wrote this haiku, about 1180 CE.

Feelings of My Thatched Hut

> *A banana plant in autumn winds--*
> *I listen to the drops of rain*
> *Fall into a basin at night.*

The rain on the banana leaves or the rustle of the wind in the banana leaves on a sunny day is garden music.

My own garden has been designed and redesigned to please the eye. I am working on growing plants with scented foliage and flowers so that fragrance is part of the experience. Thinking about banana leaves in Asian gardens reminds me that a great garden pleases the ear as well.

Sweet Potatoes, Morning Glories, and Yams

THE SWEET POTATO, *Ipomoea batatas*, is a morning glory, because it is in the genus *Ipomoea*; many of its close relatives are called morning glories. Sweet potatoes look a lot like the weedy morning glories that annoy gardeners in the southern United States. It has pale flowers with purple centers that open early in the morning and close by midday. It is a vine, with, originally, more-or-less heart-shaped leaves.

Sweet potatoes are native to the Americas and were one of the earliest plants to be domesticated. Sweet potatoes have been found at sites in Peru dated to 8,000-10,000 BCE. They were in widespread cultivation in both Mexico and Peru by 2,500 BCE.

Columbus encountered sweet potatoes and was the first to take them to Europe.

Sweet potatoes document ancient Pacific travels.

The sweet potatoes Columbus found in the Caribbean were quite starchy, but soon after, Spanish explorers in the Andes were introduced to sweeter varieties. Both types were quickly accepted by cultures in Africa and Asia. Europe was slower to adopt them, because sweet potatoes need a long growing season and cannot survive frost. Tubers were produced in Italy, Spain, and Greece, but not in England or Germany. In contrast, people in tropical Africa and Asia found them easy to grow. Today they are grown all around the world in the tropics and subtropics.

Recently, varieties of sweet potato with colorful leaves have become popular as ground covers and ornamentals. You never know where you'll meet a sweet potato these days.

Sweet Potatoes in Hawaii and Polynesia

Sweet potato culture forms an important part of the traditions of Polynesia, including Hawaii. Hawaii is the most distant group of islands in the world—2,400 miles from the nearest continent and 1,313 miles from the nearest island (Midway). Consequently, every Hawaiian plant has an interesting story, because it came a very long way. Polynesians settled in Hawaii at least 1,500 years ago, bringing sweet potatoes with them. In Hawaii and elsewhere across the islands of the Pacific—Oceania—there is clear archaeological evidence of sweet potatoes well before European contact (Magellan's voyages, 1520s).

Since sweet potatoes are native to Central and South America, this posed a problem to botanists: the Pacific is huge, how did sweet potatoes reach Hawaii and Polynesia? Sweet potatoes aren't coastal morning glories that might float to Hawaii. In fact, they've been in cultivation so long that they don't make many good seeds, so scenarios of the seeds sticking to something and riding off to a Pacific island are highly improbable as well.

A yam is not necessarily a sweet potato.

And yet, not only are they found at archaeological sites all across the Pacific from 1200 CE and earlier, but the names given them in Oceania and South America are similar. The word for sweet potato in northwestern South America (from Quechua, the language of the Inca) is *kumara, cumar* or *cumal*. Polynesians called their sweet potatoes *kuumala* and related terms (*kumara* in Maori, *'uala* in Hawaiian). Transferring a name requires human contact.

Since the 1940s botanists and ethnographers have wrestled with not believing nonwestern sailors could have traveled between South American and Polynesia even though the sweet potato clearly did.

Another line of evidence supporting contact between people in South American and Oceania, probably before 500 CE, appeared in 2013. Researchers from France, headed by Caroline Roullier, collected sweet potatoes across the Pacific and in Central and South America and compared their DNA. They also compared DNA from the oldest sweet potatoes they could find, plants that were collected and dried between 1600 and 1900. They knew that repeated movement of sweet potatoes over the last 300 years had confused the situation. Nevertheless, they added two substantial points to the argument for exchange long before European contact. First, sweet potatoes from the eastern Pacific (Hawaii, Pitcairn, and French Polynesia) were genetically similar to sweet potatoes in northern South America, where the names matched. Sweet potatoes from Mexico or the Caribbean, where sweet potatoes were called *camotil* or *camote*, were not so similar to eastern-Pacific sweet potatoes. Secondly, the preserved sweet potatoes, collected by the earliest European explorers, especially Captain Cook's first voyage in 1569, were *kumara*-type sweet potatoes, not *camote*. The authors concluded that sweet potatoes domesticated in the Americas have been brought to the islands of the Pacific repeatedly, and that the earliest was hundreds of years before European sailing ships arrived.

Open ocean navigation has become a major interest in Hawaii since the time that I lived there more than thirty years ago. There are fascinating displays now about the ways Polynesian navigators guided ships far from land, and increasingly, people are recreating those voyages. Pretty clearly, they could and did sail to Ecuador or Colombia and back.

The sweet potato's distribution alerts us to long-distance travel across the Pacific by humans, which is something we might otherwise know nothing about.

Sweet Potatoes and Yams

In moving all around the world, sweet potatoes encountered and became confused with yams.

Sweet potatoes are members of a big genus of vines, *Ipomoea* with edible below ground tubers. A few other morning glories also produce underground tubers. But morning glory tubers are not necessarily edible. The bush morning glory (*Ipomoea leptophylla*)'s tuber is solidly woody and you need a saw to cut it open unless it is very young. The morning glory Indian potato (*Ipomoea pandurata*) of the southeast United States, was noted in many books as edible, but morning glory expert Dan Austin argued persuasively that that was the result of historical authors confusing it with other plants. Native Americans used it as a purgative and did not eat it. I don't believe the tuber of any *Ipomoea* species except *Ipomoea batatas*, sweet potato, was routinely eaten by anyone.

Another big genus of vines, *Dioscorea*, is found across the tropics and has edible tubers. These plants are classified in the pantropical family Dioscoreaceae, which is not closely related to sweet potatoes. While *Ipomoea batatas* is native to the Americas, there are species of *Dioscorea* with edible tubers in Central and South America, Africa, and tropical Asia. In all three areas, *Dioscorea* species have been in cultivation since at least 3,000 BCE. Yam is the common name for plants in the genus *Dioscorea*.

Columbus was familiar with yams, so when he first saw a sweet potato, he called it a yam. Yams, *Dioscorea*, have been important foods in Africa for thousands of years and were deeply rooted in the culture, ritual, and religion of several areas. Undoubtedly slaves brought to the Americas ate sweet potatoes the way they had eaten yams in Africa.

Yam leaves

Over the years, the edible tubers of sweet potatoes and yams have been bred into all sorts of sizes and colors. A yam can look a lot like a sweet potato, or vice versa.

Wikipedia currently states that to reduce confusion, United States markets must mark sweet potatoes as sweet potatoes, even if they also call them yams. I have never seen yams (*Dioscorea*) for sale in a United States mainland grocery store. All the tubers called yams I've seen for sale have been sweet potatoes. That's why I use the scientific name after the common name here. Yam is a common name for two different plants.

In southern China in 2009, I finally saw yams, *Dioscorea*, growing. And in 2010, to my surprise, I found a Chinese yam plant, *Dioscorea polystachya*, for sale from an herb supplier in the United States. Of course I bought it and put it in my garden. It twined up the support and then up the sunflower, but did not flower. It surprised me by coming up in subsequent years. The veins of the *Dioscorea* leaf are distinctive, but otherwise it was "any small vine." The confusion with *Ipomoea* is understandable.

Perennially Popular Peonies

PEONIES! WONDERFUL BIG FLOWERS with a rich scent. No wonder they are international favorites.

Peonies are plants of the genus *Paeonia*. It is the only genus in the peony family, the Paeoniaceae. There are 33 species, very like each other and not like much of anything else. They have an odd distribution: two species are native to the western United States, a few other species are found in southern Europe and across Asia, but most peonies are native to eastern Asia.

Peonies were beloved by the Chinese.

In Asia

The Chinese have been cultivating peonies for more than 3,000 years, with written records from the early Zhou Dynasty, 1,046-256 BCE, creating hybrids, doubles, and new colors. The Chinese particularly like tree peonies (*mǔdan*), which are native only to China and available but not particularly common elsewhere, but they also love herbaceous peonies (*sháoyào*).

The Chinese *Book of Odes* (7th or 8th century BCE) includes a poem which, at the end of each stanza, describes couples exchanging *sháoyào* peony flowers The properties ascribed to peonies as binding herbs probably played into choosing them to exchange, adding symbolism (or magic) that strengthened a relationship. Or so says Needham. I can read it as some sort of euphemism.

'Beyond the Wei [River],
The ground is large and fit for pleasure.'
So the gentlemen and ladies
Make sport together,
Presenting one another with small peonies.'
(*The Qin and the Wen*, The Book of Odes.)

Peonies feature in traditional Chinese medicine, using the roots as a tonic for their astringency and as a general remedy for diseases in women.

In art, peonies represent spring, with all the symbolism typical of spring such as birth, rebirth, hope, and renewal, and consequently are a frequent motif.

The Tang Dynasty, 618-960 CE, was a period of relative peace, and both nobles and commoners took up growing peonies in a big way. The prices commanded by rare peonies could reach the equivalent of a hundred bushels of rice! A famous poem by Bai Juyi (772-846) read in part:

"For the fine flower, --a hundred pieces of damask;
For the cheap flower, --five bits of silk."
(from Needham, p. 399)

More than a thousand years ago, the Chinese wrote monograph after monograph, describing the transport, planting, grafting, pruning, and more, of peonies. Peony gardening popularity waxed and waned of course, but hundreds of cultivars were produced.

Sháoyào peonies were introduced to Japan by the 8th century CE, where the Japanese developed distinctive shapes and styles of their own.

Europeans sent reports of Chinese peonies to Europe almost immediately after reaching China by sea in the 1500s. In the 1770s, Pierre-Martial Cibot, a Jesuit missionary, wrote extensively about the beauty of Chinese peonies. He also expressed astonishment at superstitious practices in their cultivation; for example, transplanting only at the correct phase of the moon and waiting for auspicious days for other garden tasks involving peonies.

European peonies were believed to glow at night

The earliest known Chinese peony plants to actually reach western Europe arrived in 1784, by way of Siberia and Russia; other imports very soon followed. Europeans embraced them as wonderful "thornless roses." By 1884 hundreds of varieties were available in England.

Writing about 860 CE, Li Chao said:

> 'The nobility and gentry of the capital city have been making excursions to admire the peonies for about thirty years past. Every evening in spring-time the carriages and horses take madly to the roads, it being considered shameful not to spend some leisure in enjoying them." (Needham, p. 399)

Well?

Take madly to the roads and enjoy the peonies!

In Europe

In Europe, people have been using two native peonies—the female peony, *Paeonia officinalis* and the male peony, *P. mascula*—medicinally for centuries.

It is not obvious today why they are called male and female. It does not reflect the botany. Both are male, in the sense of having pollen (sperm) and both are female, in the sense of having eggs within ovules that develop into seeds. In both species, both male and female function occur within the same flower (hermaphrodite flowers). Furthermore, that explanation is relatively recent; that plants do any kind of sexual reproduction was one of Linneaus's absolutely shocking suggestions in the late 1700s. Peonies were called male and female long before that.

The Bynums in *Remarkable Plants* suggest that the designation reflects the relative size and vigor of plants of the two species, male peonies being larger than female peonies. Female peony was the plant of choice for European herbal medicine from the time of Dioscorides (64 CE) and it was used for both men's and women's problems. Any other significance seems lost to history. Today those are just the common names for the plants.

The name peony itself comes from ancient Greece. It is certainly named after Paeon, physician of the gods and god of healing. I can't confirm the more dramatic tale, often repeated, that, when the Greek god of medicine and healing, Asclepius, became dangerously jealous of his student Paeon, Zeus protected Paeon by turning him into the (important medical) plant, the peony. Websites talking about peonies give that story, but not sites about Paeon or Asclepius.

Peonies, especially the female peonies, were important medicinal plants used for an array of conditions, especially the "falling sickness" (epilepsy or other seizures). Today they are not generally recommended because of the risk of overdose, which causes severe digestive discomfort and diarrhea, and because many of the traditional usages are, in the phrasing of the *Physician's Desk Reference for Herbal Medicine*, "unproven."

As a common important medicinal, peonies have accumulated a lot of folklore. I went looking for the source of the stories or a definitive statement.

Thomas Hill, writing the first English-language garden book in 1577, wrote that if peonies are "buried or otherwise sown" around the edge of the garden, the plants "are after (as by a secret protection) preserved, that neither the great nor smaller beasts wil after spoile the plants there growing." (p. 117) Whether this has any basis, I don't know. Peonies appear on deer-resistant lists (but also on lists of plants deer like), but that is not the same thing as creating a fence that keeps beasts out.

Written and revised between 1599 and 1632, John Gerard's *Herball* is a very famous compendium of plant information, known for including plants with no medicinal value and skepticism about the more fantastic stories of his day.

Gerard wrote (I modernized the letters and the endings; "saith to said," for example):

> "There be found ... *Aglaophotides* [it means approximately "brightly shining"] described by Aelianus in his Book 14 ... That of the earth, said he, which by another name is called *Cynospastus*, lies hid in the day time among other herbs and is not known at all, and in the night time is easily seen, for it shines like a star and glitters with a fiery brightness.

> "And this *Aglaophotis* of the earth, or *Cynospastus*, is *Paeonia*; for Apuleius says, that the seeds or graines of Peionie shine in the night time like a candle and that plenty of it is in the night season found and gathered by the shepherds. Theophrastus and Pliny do show that Peionie is gathered in the night, which AElianus also affirms..."(Gerard, p. 983)

My peonies are mostly doubles, but I have never thought they shone in the night. The white ones are very visible in the dark, but no more so than white roses. Certainly they do not shine like a candle. Look for yourself and let me know!

Gerard further wrote:

> "...Aelianus said that *Cynospastus* [peony] is not plucked up without danger and that it is reported how he that first touched it, not knowing the nature thereto, perished. Therefore a string must be fastened to it in the night and a hungry dog tied thereto, who being allured by the smell of roasted flesh, set towards him, may pluck it up by the roots. Iosephus also wrote that [peony] does shine in the evening like the day star and that they who come near and pluck it up can hardly do so, except that either a woman's urine or her menses be poured upon it, and then so it may be plucked up at length.

> "Moreover, it is set down by the said Author, as also by Pliny and Theophrastus, that of necessity it must be gathered in the night, for if any man shall pluck off the fruit in the day time, being seen of the Woodpecker, he is in danger to lose his eyes; and if he cut the root, it is a chance if his fundament [buttocks or anus] fall not out. The like fabulous tale has been set forth of Mandrake, the which I have partly touched in the same chapter. But all these things are most vain and frivolous: for the root of Peionie, as also the Mandrake, may be removed at any time of the year, day or hour whatsoever." (p. 983)

I cannot find a translation of either Theophrastus or Aelian to compare, but Fraser, *Folklore of the Old Testament*, further reports that the dog that is used to pull up peony roots will die with the first light and should be buried where it falls, with certain secret rites, after which the gatherers could safely handle the peony roots. That probably comes from Aelian, although I can't confirm it.

This contrasts nicely with Cibot in the 1770s, writing disdainfully of Chinese peony superstitions. It would be fun to know how European fears of peony harvesting were lost. Gradually? Probably not simply because Gerard said so.

After the introduction of Chinese herbaceous peonies to Europe, Chinese peonies were hybridized with the European female peony, creating greater diversity of color and shape.

North America has two native species of peony, neither much in cultivation. There are likewise species in Europe and Asia known only to specialists.

Even without the rarer species, more colors and forms of peony are easily purchased than one garden can reasonably hold. Consider singles and doubles, in pinks, yellow, lavender, black and white. They are still a hit, and are generally transplanted safely in daylight.

The Quest for Fresh Ripe Pineapples

THE STORY OF PINEAPPLES reminds us of a time when you couldn't zip around the globe in an airplane.

The pineapples we see in grocery stores are the fruit of herbaceous plants, scientifically *Ananas comosus*, in the bromeliad family, Bromeliaceae. The bromeliads are almost entirely confined to the New World. Most bromeliads are epiphytes, living on trees, but pineapples grow on the ground. Pineapples were apparently domesticated prehistorically in South America and dispersed throughout all tropical America in very ancient times.

The native people of Guadalupe and other Caribbean islands considered sharing pineapples a symbol of hospitality. When Columbus landed on Guadalupe on his second voyage in 1493, they offered him pineapples. Columbus and his men thought the pineapples were delicious. Columbus called them "pine of the Indies." The men in his crew and subsequent Spaniards called pineapples *piña*, from "pine" in Spanish, apparently because it reminded them of a pine cone. The name piña or pine for pineapples carried over into English initially. In 1633, Gerard called it the pinia or pine thistle in his *Herball*.

Pineapples were among the first plants grown in glass houses

John Worledge is given credit for saying the fruit was "like a pineapple" in 1676. At that time, the word apple was used for any fruit, so a pine apple was the fruit of a pine tree, today called a pine cone. That name stuck, replacing pine of the Indies, pine thistle, and older names. Despite the shared names, pineapples are obviously not much like either pines or apples.

During the 1500s the Spanish, Portuguese, and Dutch carried pineapples all over the tropics. The plant is relatively tolerant of drought and heat and can survive quite a while under adverse conditions. As a result, it survived long sea voyages and was soon grown all over the tropical world.

From the time of Columbus, reports of how delicious pineapples are were taken back to Europe. Getting a pineapple fruit across the Atlantic without it spoiling was another thing entirely.

About 1570 one was brought to Holy Roman Emperor Charles V, but it was rotten.

Attempts to grow pineapples in northern Europe were frustrated by its requirement for warm conditions and a long growing season. Pineapples grow very slowly under cool conditions and fruit development requires more time than a northern European summer provides. The gardeners of the 1500s and early 1600s knew what they needed to do to get pineapple fruit; they simply couldn't create those conditions. The development of glasshouses (hothouses, greenhouses) was driven by that knowledge. One of the first fruits grown in the earliest glasshouses was the pineapple.

In England, the first pineapple fruit successfully grown was during Cromwell's time, 1653-1658. In 1661 a greenhouse-grown pineapple was offered to Charles II, but the English king was not impressed. Although it was a great botanical success to have gotten the plant to flower and develop a fruit in the glasshouse, the fruit did not taste very good. (As we still observe of hothouse fruits and vegetables.) A famous painting commemorates the presentation of the pineapple to King Charles. Interestingly, the existing painting is apparently an imitation of the original: *John Rose*

(1619–1677), the Royal Gardener, presenting a Pineapple to King Charles II (1630–1685) (after Henry Dankerts), by Thomas Stewart (1766 - c. 1801). (You can see it online.)

The earliest mention of pineapple in an English cookbook is in Richard Bradley's second cookbook, published in 1732, which seems to suggest that by then pineapples were not entirely a glasshouse novelty item. However, although the book says it is written for a country housewife, Bradley wrote, "To make a tart of the Ananas, or Pine-Apple. From Barbados."

The availability of good pineapple outside of the tropics is a recent result of well-regulated refrigeration and air transport. In my childhood in the 1950s, pineapple came out of cans. Only canned pineapple was widely available. Fresh pineapples were rare, very expensive, and almost always disappointing.

Refrigerated ships first made a successful trip in the 1870s, but unlike bananas, tomatoes, and apples, pineapples do not ripen after picking but simply start to deteriorate. Even refrigerated, pineapples do not survive a long sea voyage. Bringing fruits grown in the tropics to markets in North America or Europe required temperature- and air-controlled containers on fast ships or planes.

The pineapple story illustrates how far we have come in growing plants in greenhouses and in shipping fresh fruit across the world.

When you see fresh pineapple in your grocery store, think of the generations of kings in Europe who couldn't get one, no matter who they sent or what they spent.

Afterword

The plants we see or eat every day came from Europe, South America, China, and beyond. They were valued for their flavors or flowers or medicinal uses and accumulated folklore and symbolism. In many cases, much of their lore has been forgotten and the plants have simply become useful objects to busy people.

Retelling the tales and folklore, so that you know you are biting a banana finger, or can be comforted as the Hebrews were that pomegranates grow in the Promised Land, or know that you are being daring to transplant a peony in the light of day…I hope those add wonder to your garden or table.

Notes and Sources

BCE = Before Common Era = BC, Before Christ,
CE = Common Era, beginning in the year 1 = AD

Wandering Watermelons –
Sources

Bates, D. M. and R. W. Robertson. 1995. Cucumbers, melons and water-melons. Pp. 89-96 In: J. Smartt and N. W. Simmonds. The evolution of crop plants. 2nd ed. Longman Press, London.

Deane, G. Citron melon. Eat the weeds. http://tinyurl.com/h9gcef8

Hall, D. W., V.V. Vandiver and J.A.Ferrell. 1991. Citron (citron melon), *Citrullus lanatus* (Thunb.) Mats. & Nakai. University of Florida IFAS Extension http://tinyurl.com/jy7qd7z

Kiple, K. F. and K. C. Ornelas, editors. 2000. Cucumbers. The Cambridge world history of food. Cambridge University Press, Cambridge. http://tinyurl.com/kvr7je6

Needham, J. 1986. Science and civilization in China. Vol VI: 1 Botany. Cambridge University Press, Cambridge.

Paris, H. S., M-C. Daunay, and J. Janick. 2013. Medieval iconography of watermelons in Mediterranean Europe. Annals of Botany. 112: 867-879.

Valder, P. 1999. The garden plants of China. Timber Press, Portland, Oregon.

Pomegranates in Story and History –
Sources

about.com. 2015. The history of the hand grenade. http://tinyurl.com/j7s2p55

Brittanica.com. Granada. http://tinyurl.com/hvclbr4

Bynum, H. and W. Bynum. 2014. Remarkable plants that shape our world. University of Chicago Press, Chicago.

Dollinger, A. 2000. Pomegranates. An introduction to the history and culture of pharaonic Egypt.
http://tinyurl.com/hqaw8wu

Dunmire, W. W. 2004. Gardens of New Spain. University of Texas Press, Austin, Texas. Says clearly the Moors brought pomegranates to Spain.

Food Reference.com Pomegranates.
http://tinyurl.com/zotz59k
Lots more wonderful pomegranate information!

Krutch, J. W. 1976. Herbal. David R. Godine, publisher. Boston, Massachusetts.

Valder, P. 1999. The Garden plants of China. Timber Press, Portland Oregon.

Vamosh, M. F. No date given. Holy Land's food at the time of the Bible. Palphot Ltd., Herzlia, Israel.

van Wyk, B-E. 2005. Food plants of the world. Timber Press, Portland, Oregon.

Camellia and Tea –
Sources

American Camellia Society
http://tinyurl.com/hbd8o99

Duke, J. A. 1983. *Camellia sinensis* (L.) Kuntz. Handbook of energy crops.
http://tinyurl.com/a7bz9

Ellis, R. T. 1997. Tea, *Camellia sinensis* (Camelliaceae). Pp. 22-27. In J. Smartt and N. W. Simmonds, The evolution of crop plants, 2nd ed. Longman Press, London.

Lauener, L. A. 1996.The introduction of Chinese plants into Europe. D. K. Ferguson, editor. SPB Academic Publishing, London.

Ming, T-T, and W-J. Zhang. 1996. The evolution and distribution of genus *Camellia*, Acta Botanica Yunnanica. 18 (1): 1-13. http://tinyurl.com/jvajxjp

Simpson, B. B. and M. C. Orgazaly. 2001. Economic botany. 3rd. ed. McGraw-Hill, Boston.

Chocolate: Food of the Gods –
Sources

Coe, S. D. and M. D. Coe. 2000. The true history of chocolate. Thames & Hudson, London.

Simpson, B.B. and M. C. Orgazaly. 2001. Economic botany. 3rd ed. McGraw-Hill, New York.

Try mole:

Allrecipes.com. 2016. Mole sauce. http://allrecipes.com/recipes/16084/side-dish/sauces-and-condiments/sauce

Chrysanthemum: The Quintessential Plant of Fall –
Sources

Miles, T. 2004. Chrysanthemum. Bellarmine University. http://tinyurl.com/jrgj47v

Needham, J. 1986. Science and civilization in China. VI: 1 Botany. Cambridge University Press, Cambridge.

Valder, P. 1999. The garden plants of China. Timber Press, Portland, Oregon.

Welch, P. B. 2008. Chinese art. A guide to motifs and visual imagery. Tuttle Press, Tokyo.

Not Plain Vanilla –
Sources

Coe, S. D. 1994. America's first cuisines. University of Texas Press, Austin, Texas.

Emmart, E. W. translator & editor. 1940. The Badianus manuscript. (An Aztec herbal of 1552). Johns Hopkins Press, Baltimore.

Rain, P. "Vanilla: nectar of the gods." Pp. 35-46 In: N. Foster and L. S. Cordell. 1992. Chilies to chocolate. Food the Americas gave the world. The University of Arizona Press, Tucson, Arizona.

Proctor, M. and P. Yeo. 1973. The pollination of flowers. Collins, London.

Simpson, B. B. and M. C. Orgazaly. 2001. Economic botany, 3rd ed. McGraw-Hill, New York.

Swain, J. O. 1991. The lore of spices. Crescent Books, Gothenberg, Sweden.

Wilson, C.A. 1991. Food and drink in Britain. Academy Chicago Publishers, Chicago.

Holly, Celebrating the Solstice and Christmas for Millennia –

Notes

Fruit and drupe: Fruit is a good general word for plant parts that contain seeds. Long ago, botanists compared the detailed structure of fruits and created technical words that help in identifying plants; words like pome, drupe, and silique. They defined a berry as a "simple fleshy fruit with more than one seed"; for example, a grape. Drupes are usually one-seeded fleshy fruits with a hard inner fruit coat. Holly fruits have only one seed and a hard layer around the seed inside the fruit, so properly, holly "berries" are drupes. Clearly, berry is a common non-technical term for lots of small round fruits that have other technical names. What I'd say is that there are two definitions for "berry," one botanical and one popular. Just consider your audience when you choose the word berry.

Sources

Barcus, C. U. 2012. Hollies get prickly for a reason
http://tinyurl.com/d3tzj6b

California Invasive Plant Control. 2006. *Ilex aquifolium* English holly. http://tinyurl.com/jskyoxv

Danin, A. (ed.) 2006+, {continuously updated}. Flora of Israel online. The Hebrew University of Jerusalem, Jerusalem, Israel. http://tinyurl.com/2hoj8a

Kirchheimer, S. No date given. The history of the holly plant. Gardenguides.com. http://tinyurl.com/hpmy9hw

Murrell, D. 2008. Superstitions. 1013 of the wackiest myths, fables and old wives' tales. Amber Books, Ltd., New York.

Obeso, J. R. 1997. The induction of spinescence in European holly leaves by browsing ungulates. Plant Ecology. 129: 149-156.

Plants in the Bible, Old Dominion University plant website http://tinyurl.com/njr3zqd

Pollington, S. 2000. Leechcraft. Early English charms, plantlore and healing. Anglo-Saxon Books, London.

Raven, P. H., R. F. Evert and S. E. Eichhorn. 1992. Biology of plants. 5th ed. Worth Publishing, New York.

Rich, V. 1998. Cursing the basil and other folklore of the garden. Horsdal and Schubart, Winnepeg.

Vickery, R. 1993. Oxford dictionary of plant lore. Oxford University Press, Oxford.

Holly Postscript –
Sources

Cahill, L. How did Hollywood get its name? blog.treepeople.org. http://tinyurl.com/z73v8pv

Daeida Hartle Wilcox Beveridge (1862-1914)--from Hicksville to Hollywood. Hicksville Historical Society, Inc. http://tinyurl.com/gnvttvs

Heteromeles arbutifolia Lady Bird Johnson Wildflower Center. http://tinyurl.com/j6top3h

Hightower, S. *Heteromeles arbutifolia*-toyon. Sonoma master gardener. http://tinyurl.com/hq32g8j

History of Hollywood, Illinois.
  http://tinyurl.com/zj2hxs7
"Holly, n.," Oxford English Dictionary online. Hollywood,
  Florida history http://tinyurl.com/gmpqbbs
"Holy, n., adj." Oxford English Dictionary online.
Johnson, T. 2011. Helping holly survive past Christmas.
  http://tinyurl.com/z6xflwv
Keith, G. W. Margaret Virginia (Gigi) Whitley's diary
  naming of Hollywood 1886. The father of Hollywood
  website. Accessed 2014. http://tinyurl.com/hpwp2f7
Water and Power Associates History
  http://tinyurl.com/gvzca6u

The Coconuts of Medieval Iceland –
Sources
Harries, H. C. 1995. Coconut. *Cocos nucifera* L. (Palmae).
  Pp. 389-394 In: J. Smartt and N. W. Simmonds, The
  evolution of crop plants, 2nd ed. Longman Press, London.
Simpson, B.B. and M. C. Ogorzaly. 2014. Economic Botany:
  Plants in our world. 4th ed. McGraw-Hill, New York.
Vaughan, J.G. and C. A. Geissler. 1997. The new Oxford
  book of food plants. Oxford University Press, Oxford.

The Exquisite Lotus –
Sources
Bynum, H. and W. Bynum. 2014. Remarkable plants that
  shape our world. University of Chicago Press, Chicago.
Gupta, S. M. 1996. Plants in Indian temple art. B. R.
  Publishing Corporation, Delhi.
Missouri Botanical Garden. Missouri Plant Finder.
  Nelumbo lutea. http://www.missouribotanicalgarden.
  http://tinyurl.com/zaltp6e
Stevens, P. F. 2001 onwards. Nelumbonaceae. Angiosperm
  phylogeny website. http://tinyurl.com/f746l
Vaughan, J. G. and C. A. Geissler. 1997. The new Oxford
  book of food plants. Oxford University Press, Oxford.

Wang, C. 2010. Seriously Asian: Lotus root recipe.
http://tinyurl.com/2vkf9k3

Common Houseleek and its Folklore –
Sources
Bosworth, J. An Anglo-Saxon Dictionary Online. *Leác*. Ed.
Thomas Northcote Toller. Charles University, Prague,
March 21, 2010. http://tinyurl.com/h9rrk9e
Capilulare de villis translation: University of Leicester
http://tinyurl.com/h9h7fo2
Clotfelter, S. 2013. High Park fire anniversary is a reminder
to prep disaster kit. The Denver Post. June 8, 2013.
http://tinyurl.com/hpttum3
Coombes, A. J. 1985. Dictionary of plant names. Timber
Press, Portland, Oregon.
Culpeper, N. 1652. Culpeper's complete herbal.
http://tinyurl.com/h2jluao
Gerard, J. 1597. The herball or generall historie of plantes. K.
Stuber. 2007. Wageningen UR Library Publisher.
Grieve, M. 1971 (originally 1931). A modern herbal. Dover
Publications, New York, New York.
Kelaidis, G. M. 2008. Hardy succulents. Storey Publishing,
North Adams, Massachusetts.
Mabey, R., ed. 1987. The gardener's labyrinth of Thomas
Hill. Oxford University Press, Oxford. [reproduction of
the first popular gardening manual, 1577].

A World of Bananas –
Sources
Bynum, H. and W. Bynum. 2014. Remarkable plants that
shape our world. The University of Chicago Press,
Chicago.
Hinton, D. 2008.Classic Chinese Poetry: An Anthology
https://books.google.com/
Katsev, I. 2007-2016. Banana. http://tinyurl.com/zvpsf42

National Geographic. 2008. Edible, an illustrated guide to the world's food plants. National Geographic Society, Washington, D.C.

Oxford English Dictionary. "Banana, n."

Sanders, A. No date given. How tall is a banana tree? http://tinyurl.com/gwvf7ac

Shively, D. H. 2011. "Basho--The Man and the Plant" in *Harvard Journal of Asiatic Studies*, v. 16, no., 1-2, 1953. p. 146-161. Online at The hermitary and Meng hu http://tinyurl.com/jb5mnkn

Simmonds, N. W. 1995. Bananas Musa (Musaceae). pp. 370-375 In J. Smartt and N. W. Simmonds. Evolution of crop plants, 2nd ed. Longman, London.

Statistica.com Global fruit production in 2013, by variety (in million metric tons). http://tinyurl.com/hdoqwbw

Valder, P. 1999. The garden plants of China. Timber Press, Portland, Oregon.

Van Wyk, B-E. 2005. Food plants of the world. Timber Press, Portland, Oregon.

Vaughan, J. G. and C. A. Geissler. 1997. The new Oxford book of food plants. Oxford University Press, Oxford.

Sweet Potatoes, Morning Glories, and Yams – Sources

Austin, D. F. 2011. Indian potato (*Ipomoea pandurata, Convolvulaceae*)—a record of confusion. *Economic Botany*. 65 (4):48-421.

Bohac, J. R., P. D. Dukes, and D. F. Austin. 1995. Sweet potato, *Ipomoea batatas* (Convolvulaceae). Pp. 57- 62 In: J. Smartt and N. W. Simmonds. 1995. The evolution of crop plants. Longman Press, London.

Hahn, S. K. "Yams, *Dioscorea* spp. (Dioscoreaceae). Pp. 112-120 In: J. Smartt and N. W. Simmonds. 1995. The evolution of crop plants. Longman Press, London.

Harkins, J. G. and J. Francisco-Ortega. 1993. The early history of the potato in Europe. *Euphytica*. 70: 1-7.

Roullier, C., L. Benoit, D. B. McKey, and V. Lebot. 2013. Historical collections reveal patterns of diffusion of sweet potato in Oceania obscured by modern plant movements and recombination. Proceedings of the National Academy of Sciences, USA. 110 (6): 2205-2210.

Peonies –
Sources

Bynum, H. and W. Bynum. 2014. Remarkable plants that shape our world. The University of Chicago Press, Chicago.

Fraser, J. G. 1919. Folklore of the Old Testament, Vol 2. MacMillan. http://tinyurl.com/zn8qeoa

Gerard, J. 1636. Chap. 380. Peionie. The Herball http://tinyurl.com/zhagtej

In Defense of Plants. 2016. America's native peonies. http://tinyurl.com/jv57qnc

Lauener, L.A. 1996. The introduction of Chinese plants into Europe. SPB Academic Publishing, Amsterdam.

Li, S.-C. 1973. Chinese medicinal herbs. A modern edition of a classic sixteenth-century manual. Dover Press, Mineola, New York.

Mabey, R., ed. 1987. The gardener's labyrinth of Thomas Hill. Oxford University Press, Oxford. [reproduction of the first popular gardening manual, 1577]

Needham, J. 1986. Science and civilization in China. Vol VI: 1 Botany. Cambridge University Press, Cambridge.

PDR (Physician's Desk Reference) for herbal medicine. 2007. 4th ed. Thomson Healthcare, Inc., Montvale, New Jersey.

Valder, P. 1999. The garden plants of China. Timber Press, Portland, Oregon.

The Qin and the Wen. The book of odes. Full poem in English and Chinese. http://tinyurl.com/hcaf43u

The Quest for Fresh Ripe Pineapples –
Sources

Bradley, R. 1732. The country housewife and lady's director in the management of a house, and the delights and profits of a farm. Published by Richard Bradley. Online at http://tinyurl.com/gnhcw6h.

Foster, N. and L. S. Cordell. 1992. Chilies to chocolate: Food the Americas gave the world. University of Arizona Press, Tucson, Arizona.

Gerard, John. 1975. The herbal or general history of plants. Complete 1633 edition as revised and enlarged by Thomas Johnson. Dover Publications, New York, New York. (Pineapples only appear in the 1633 edition, not the 1597 edition.)

Kiple, K.F. and K. C. Ornelas. 2000. The Cambridge world history of food. Cambridge University Press, Cambridge.

Leal, F. 1997. Pineapple, *Ananas comosus* (Bromeliaceae), Pp. 19-22 In: J. Smartt and N. W. Simmonds. The evolution of crop plants. 2nd ed. Longman Press, London.

Oxford English Dictionary. "apple, n.", "pine apple, n." Oxford English dictionary online. Website http://tinyurl.com/j2xxlsl

Simpson, Beryl B. and Molly C. Orgazaly. 2001. Economic botany. McGraw-Hill, Boston, Massachusetts.

A Wandering Botanist visits Bali

Read more on my website awanderingbotanist.com or blog khkeeler.blogspot.com.

My previous book, *Curious Stories of Familiar Garden Plants*, is available at Amazon.com.

www.ingramcontent.com/pod-product-compliance
Lightning Source LLC
Chambersburg PA
CBHW040127270326
41927CB00001B/7